TRAVIS KELCE

DEREK MOON

Apex is distributed by North Star Editions:
sales@northstareditions.com | 888-417-0195

Produced for Apex by Red Line Editorial.

Photographs ©: Ryan Kang/AP Images, cover, 1; Perry Knotts/Getty Images Sport/Getty Images, 4–5, 56–57; Patrick Smith/Getty Images Sport/Getty Images, 6–7; Shutterstock Images, 8–9; David Calvert/American Century Investments/Getty Images Entertainment/Getty Images, 10–11; Kevin Mazur/Roc Nation/Getty Images Entertainment/Getty Images, 12–13; Al Behrman/AP Images, 14–15, 22–23; Michael Allio/Icon Sportswire/AP Images, 16–17; Jim McIsaac/Getty Images Sport/Getty Images, 18–19; Andy Lyons/Getty Images Sport/Getty Images, 20–21; Joe Robbins/Getty Images Sport/Getty Images, 24–25, 34–35; Stacy Revere/Getty Images Sport/Getty Images, 26–27; Doug Pensinger/Getty Images Sport/Getty Images, 28–29, 30–31; Scott Halleran/Getty Images Sport/Getty Images, 32–33; Aaron M. Sprecher/AP Images, 37, 58–59; Joe Sargent/Getty Images Sport/Getty Images, 38–39; Peter G. Aiken/Getty Images Sport/ Getty Images, 40–41; G. Newman Lowrance/AP Images, 42–43; Dustin Bradford/Getty Images Sport/Getty Images, 44–45; David Eulitt/Getty Images Sport/Getty Images, 46–47; Christian Petersen/Getty Images Sport/ Getty Images, 49; Ryan Kang/Getty Images Sport/Getty Images, 50–51; Michael Owens/Getty Images Sport/Getty Images, 52–53; Cooper Neill/ Getty Images Sport/Getty Images, 54–55

Library of Congress Control Number: 2024952001

ISBN
979-8-89250-724-0 (hardcover)
979-8-89250-776-9 (paperback)
979-8-89250-758-5 (ebook pdf)
979-8-89250-742-4 (hosted ebook)

Printed in the United States of America
Mankato, MN
082025

NOTE TO PARENTS AND EDUCATORS

Apex books are designed to build literacy skills in striving readers. Exciting, high-interest content attracts and holds readers' attention. The text is carefully leveled to allow students to achieve success quickly.

TABLE OF CONTENTS

CHAPTER 1

TO THE SUPER BOWL

The Kansas City Chiefs were one win from reaching the Super Bowl. The Chiefs were playing the Baltimore Ravens. Early in the game, Kansas City faced a fourth down. Travis Kelce took off running. He leaped up for a 13-yard catch. The Chiefs had a first down.

The Kansas City Chiefs played the Baltimore Ravens on January 28, 2024.

Two plays later, the Chiefs were at the 19-yard line. Kelce ran toward the end zone. Quarterback Patrick Mahomes launched a pass. Falling backward, Kelce grabbed the ball. His touchdown helped send the Chiefs to the Super Bowl.

RECORD SETTER

The Chiefs' win against the Baltimore Ravens was Travis Kelce's 21st playoff game. He snagged his 152nd postseason catch during the game. That set an NFL record.

Travis Kelce celebrates a first-quarter touchdown against the Ravens.

CHAPTER 2

CLEVELAND TO CINCINNATI

Travis Kelce was born on October 5, 1989. He was the second of two brothers. Travis's brother, Jason, is nearly two years older. The Kelce family lived in Cleveland Heights, Ohio.

As kids, Travis and Jason played and competed a lot. The brothers had plenty of fun. But sometimes they got into trouble. Travis even got kicked out of preschool. Sports became a good way to let out his energy.

COACH KELCE

Early on, Ed Kelce helped coach his sons. He coached the boys' little league baseball teams. The three often practiced sports at home, too.

Ed Kelce (left) is Travis's dad. Ed played football in high school.

Travis's mom, Donna, cheered on her sons throughout their football careers.

Travis went to Cleveland Heights High School. He played three sports there. He awed teammates with dunks on the basketball court. His fastballs stood out on the baseball diamond. On the football field, Travis played quarterback. He had a strong throwing arm. But he could also gain yards on the ground.

STAR QUARTERBACK

The Cleveland Heights football team struggled in 2007. But Travis kept up his strong play. He passed for more than 1,000 yards. He also ran for more than 1,000 yards.

Many colleges took notice of Travis. Most coaches thought he should play tight end or defensive end. However, coaches at the University of Cincinnati said that he could play quarterback. Plus, Jason Kelce already played for the school. Travis decided to join his brother.

Jason Kelce (60) joined the Cincinnati Bearcats in 2006.

CHAPTER 3

BECOMING A TIGHT END

The Cincinnati Bearcats had many great players. So, Travis Kelce spent his first year on the bench. He didn't play in any games during the 2008 season. He took the time to practice and learn.

Cincinnati's football team plays at Nippert Stadium.

In 2009, coaches wanted to get Kelce on the field. So, the team came up with a set of "wildcat" plays. On these plays, Kelce was the quarterback. He could keep the ball and run. Or he could give it to a teammate. Kelce had to think fast. He appeared in only a few plays each game. But he showed promise.

TOGETHER AGAIN

Jason Kelce had arrived at Cincinnati as a walk-on. But he became a great offensive lineman. In 2009, he helped block for Travis.

The Cincinnati Bearcats went 12–1 in 2009.

The Bearcats' coach left after the 2009 season. Soon after, Kelce was caught breaking team rules. Cincinnati's new coach suspended him. Kelce missed the 2010 season. He also lost his scholarship.

Jason Kelce was a senior at the time. He invited Travis to live with him. Jason helped Travis get back on the field. But the coach said that Travis had to play tight end.

Tight ends are usually tall. At 6-foot-5 (196 cm), Travis Kelce was a good fit for the position.

Kelce's height helped him catch passes over smaller defenders.

Switching positions was difficult. Kelce had to learn how to block. He had to practice his footwork and catching, too. In 2011, he caught just 13 passes. But he kept practicing. The hard work paid off. Kelce made plays all over the field in 2012.

WHERE IS TRAVIS?

Tight ends typically line up beside the offensive line. Kelce often lined up there. But sometimes he started in the backfield. Other times, he started out wide. This created mismatches with smaller defenders.

Cincinnati played in the 2012 Belk Bowl. The score was tied with less than a minute to go. Then Kelce caught a pass near midfield. He pulled away from two defenders and scored. The 83-yard touchdown gave the Bearcats a win. Kelce ended his college career as an all-conference player. Next, he was off to the NFL Draft.

BACK TO SCHOOL

Kelce left for the NFL before graduating from the University of Cincinnati. Years later, he went back to finish his classes. Kelce earned his degree in 2022.

Kelce had 722 receiving yards in 2012. That set a Cincinnati record for tight ends.

CHAPTER 4

RISING STAR

NFL teams were unsure about Kelce. He had played only one great college season. His suspension also concerned teams. But the Kansas City Chiefs liked his skills. They knew he worked hard. So, the Chiefs chose Kelce in the third round of the draft.

Kelce had a 17-yard catch in his first preseason game with the Chiefs.

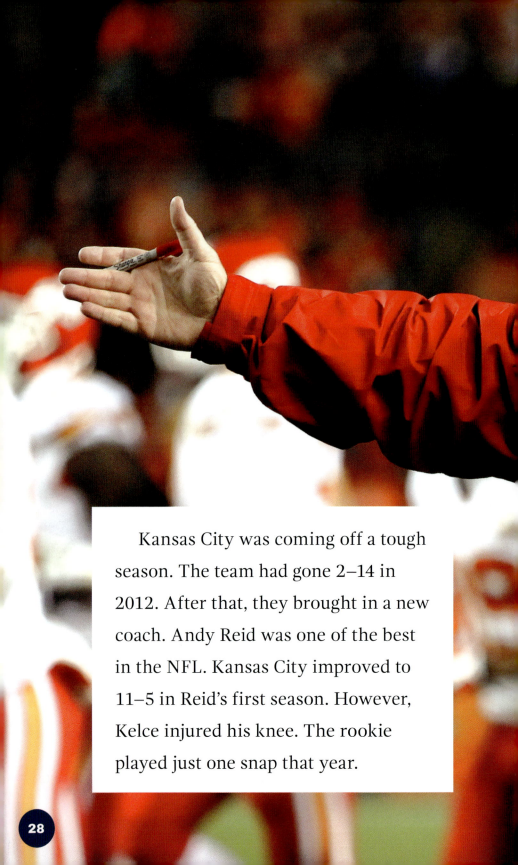

Kansas City was coming off a tough season. The team had gone 2–14 in 2012. After that, they brought in a new coach. Andy Reid was one of the best in the NFL. Kansas City improved to 11–5 in Reid's first season. However, Kelce injured his knee. The rookie played just one snap that year.

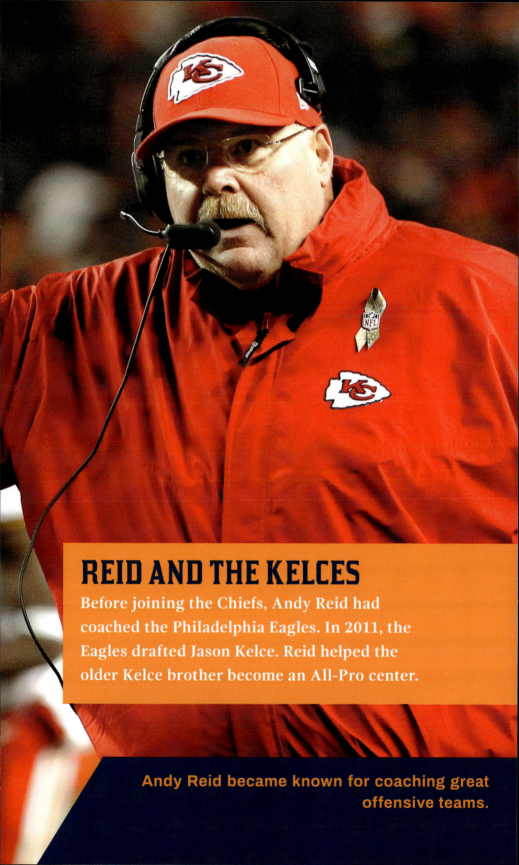

REID AND THE KELCES

Before joining the Chiefs, Andy Reid had coached the Philadelphia Eagles. In 2011, the Eagles drafted Jason Kelce. Reid helped the older Kelce brother become an All-Pro center.

Andy Reid became known for coaching great offensive teams.

Kelce got a fresh start in 2014. He showed that he could be a dependable pass catcher. In 2015, he played even better. He had 875 receiving yards. He also scored five touchdowns.

TEAM LEADER

Kelce showed off his leadership skills in the pros. He practiced hard. Teammates followed his example. Chiefs players also fed off Kelce's energy during games.

Travis Kelce pulled in 67 catches during the 2014 season.

The Chiefs posted an 11–5 record in 2015.

After the 2015 regular season, the Chiefs reached the playoffs. They hosted the Houston Texans. Kelce dominated. He caught 8 passes for 128 yards. Kansas City won 30–0. However, the Chiefs fell to the New England Patriots the next week.

CATCHING KELCE

Kelce loves to have fun. TV producers noticed. The tight end starred in a reality TV show. *Catching Kelce* was a dating show. It ran for a single season in 2016.

Kelce scored four touchdowns in the 2016 regular season.

Kelce continued to improve. In 2016, he recorded 1,125 receiving yards. That led the team. Kelce also began a streak of seven seasons with at least 1,000 yards. He had become one of the league's best tight ends. Kelce was named a first-team All-Pro.

SHOWING SUPPORT

In 2016, Colin Kaepernick began kneeling during the national anthem. The San Francisco 49ers quarterback wanted to bring attention to unfair police treatment of Black people. In 2017, Kelce knelt, too. He wanted to show his support.

CHRISTMAS PARTY

The Chiefs played the Denver Broncos on Christmas Day in 2016. Travis Kelce gave the Kansas City fans a memorable night. His biggest play came late in the first quarter.

Quarterback Alex Smith threw Kelce a short pass. The tight end made the most of it. He darted between several defenders. Then he made it to the open field. Kelce ran 80 yards for a touchdown. By the end of the game, he had 160 receiving yards. Kansas City won 33–10.

KELCE FINISHED THE BRONCOS GAME WITH 11 CATCHES.

CHAPTER 5

CHAMPION CHIEFS

In 2018, Patrick Mahomes took over as the Chiefs' quarterback. By Week 2, he had a new favorite target. Kelce caught seven passes in that game. They included touchdowns of 19 and 25 yards.

Kelce had 109 receiving yards in the Chiefs' Week 2 win over the Pittsburgh Steelers.

Mahomes had a strong arm. His vision and creativity set him apart, too. Mahomes often passed to Kelce. Each player always seemed to know what the other would do. After the 2018 regular season, the duo led the Chiefs to the conference title game. Kansas City lost in overtime. But Kelce wasn't finished.

TRICKY TIGHT END

Even though he played tight end, Kelce had the mind of a quarterback. He often recognized the defense's plan. Then, he changed his route mid-play. He found open spots all over the field.

After the 2018 season, Kelce had 10 catches in the playoffs.

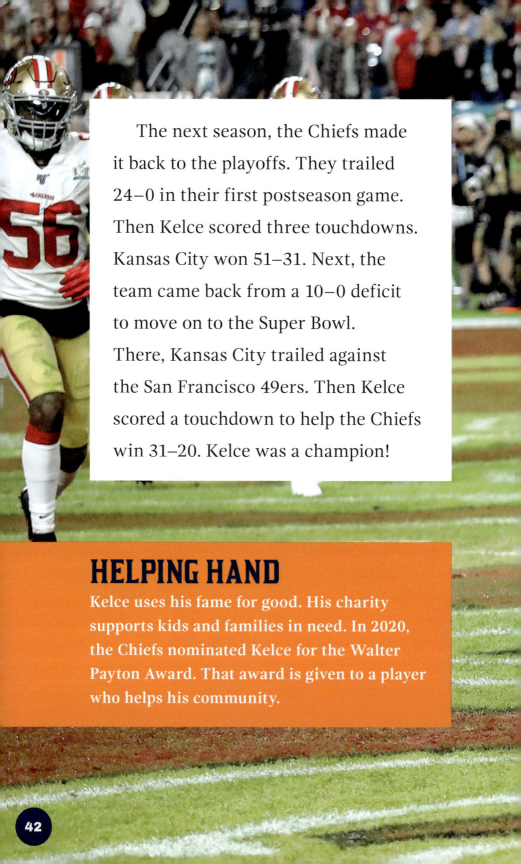

The next season, the Chiefs made it back to the playoffs. They trailed 24–0 in their first postseason game. Then Kelce scored three touchdowns. Kansas City won 51–31. Next, the team came back from a 10–0 deficit to move on to the Super Bowl. There, Kansas City trailed against the San Francisco 49ers. Then Kelce scored a touchdown to help the Chiefs win 31–20. Kelce was a champion!

HELPING HAND

Kelce uses his fame for good. His charity supports kids and families in need. In 2020, the Chiefs nominated Kelce for the Walter Payton Award. That award is given to a player who helps his community.

Kelce scored a touchdown in the fourth quarter of the Super Bowl.

Kelce had 1,416 receiving yards in 2020. That set an NFL record for tight ends.

Kelce's big plays helped the Chiefs reach another Super Bowl in the 2020 season. This time, they lost to the Tampa Bay Buccaneers The next year, Kansas City had another playoff run. They reached the conference title game. But the Cincinnati Bengals won the game in overtime.

13 SECONDS

In the 2021 season, Kansas City played the Buffalo Bills in an epic playoff game. The Chiefs trailed by three points. Only 13 seconds remained in the game. But Kelce made a clutch catch. It put the Chiefs in field-goal range. The kick was good. Then, Kelce scored the winning touchdown in overtime.

During the 2022 regular season, Kelce had 110 catches and 12 touchdowns. Both were career highs. But he saved his best game for the playoffs. Kelce caught 14 passes in a win over the Jacksonville Jaguars. That was a playoff record for tight ends. After beating the Bengals in the next round, the Chiefs moved on to another Super Bowl.

Kelce grabbed two touchdown passes in the Chiefs' playoff win against Jacksonville.

THE KELCE BOWL

After the 2022 regular season, Kansas City met the Philadelphia Eagles in the Super Bowl. That meant Travis Kelce played Jason Kelce. It was the first time that brothers faced off in the Super Bowl.

Both brothers were among the best at their positions. But Travis left the game with bragging rights. He had six catches. One of them was an 18-yard touchdown. It opened the scoring for Kansas City. The Chiefs won the game 38–35.

TRAVIS KELCE RECORDED 81 RECEIVING YARDS IN THE SUPER BOWL.

CHAPTER 6

ALL-TIME GREAT

By 2023, Patrick Mahomes had become one of the league's top quarterbacks. However, Kansas City's receivers sometimes struggled to get open. Kelce was the exception.

Kelce became known for great route-running.
He could separate from defenders.

Kelce missed two games in 2023. But he still led the Chiefs in receiving yards during the regular season. Then he scored two touchdowns in the Chiefs' second playoff game. Kelce followed that by catching 11 passes in the conference title game. The season ended with another comeback win in the Super Bowl.

TAYLOR SWIFT

In 2023, Kelce began dating singer Taylor Swift. They quickly became one of the most famous celebrity couples in the world. Cameras often showed Swift at games. Many of her fans started watching football, too.

On February 11, 2024, the Chiefs beat the San Francisco 49ers 25–22 to win the Super Bowl.

Kelce had a slow start to the 2024 season. He did not score a touchdown until Week 8. But the Chiefs still found ways to win. They lost only two games during the season. That gave Kansas City a No. 1 seed in the playoffs.

PODCAST HOSTS

Travis and Jason Kelce still have a close relationship. Many fans enjoy listening to their conversations on *New Heights*. It became one of the most popular podcasts.

Kelce had 100 receiving yards in an overtime win against the Tampa Bay Buccaneers.

Once again, Kelce stepped up in the playoffs. First, he piled up 117 receiving yards and a touchdown against the Houston Texans. Then came the conference championship game. Defenders stayed on Kelce. That attention opened up the field for other receivers. Kansas City moved on to a third straight Super Bowl. The Chiefs lost to the Eagles. But Kelce had been an important part of the team's historic run.

Kelce took a pass 49 yards against the Houston Texans.

TIMELINE

1989

2008

2012

2013

2020

Travis Kelce is born in Westlake, Ohio, on October 5.

In his final college game, Kelce scores an 83-yard touchdown to help Cincinnati win the Belk Bowl.

On February 2, Kelce helps Kansas City win its first Super Bowl in 50 years.

Travis Kelce begins attending the University of Cincinnati.

The Kansas City Chiefs select Kelce in the third round of the NFL Draft.

2020

2023

2023

2024

2024

On January 21, Kelce hauls in 14 catches against the Jacksonville Jaguars, setting a new playoff record for tight ends.

On February 11, Kelce records nine catches to help the Chiefs win their third Super Bowl in five years.

On December 27, Kelce reaches 1,416 receiving yards for the season, setting a record for tight ends.

On February 12, the Chiefs beat Jason Kelce and the Philadelphia Eagles in the Super Bowl.

Kelce makes the Pro Bowl for the 10th year in a row.

COMPREHENSION QUESTIONS

Write your answers on a separate piece of paper.

1. Write a paragraph that explains the main ideas of Chapter 2.

2. What do you think is Travis Kelce's most impressive accomplishment? Why?

3. Which team did the Kansas City Chiefs beat in Kelce's first Super Bowl appearance?
   A. Buffalo Bills
   B. Philadelphia Eagles
   C. San Francisco 49ers

4. How many seasons did Kelce play tight end for the Cincinnati Bearcats?
   A. two
   B. three
   C. four

5. What does **dominated** mean in this book?

*Kelce **dominated**. He caught 8 passes for 128 yards. Kansas City won 30–0.*

    A. ran more slowly than defenders

    B. played much better than others

    C. had trouble catching the ball

6. What does **target** mean in this book?

*In 2018, Patrick Mahomes took over as the Chiefs' quarterback. By Week 2, he had a new favorite **target**. Kelce caught seven passes in that game.*

    A. something aimed at

    B. something avoided

    C. something to catch

Answer key on page 64.

GLOSSARY

All-Pro
One of the best players at a given position in the NFL.

charity
A group that gives help to people in need.

conference
A group of teams that make up part of a sports league.

draft
A system that lets teams select new players coming into the league.

nominated
Chose someone as a finalist for an award or honor.

overtime
An extra period that happens if two teams are tied at the end of the fourth quarter.

producers
People who help plan the making of movies or TV shows.

rookie
An athlete in his or her first year as a professional player.

scholarship
Money given to someone to help pay for college.

suspended
Decided that someone was not allowed to take part in something for a certain period of time.

walk-on
A college athlete who isn't offered a scholarship but still makes a team.

TO LEARN MORE

BOOKS

Coleman, Ted. *Kansas City Chiefs All-Time Greats.* Press Box Books, 2022.

Labrecque, Ellen. *Who Is Travis Kelce?* Penguin Workshop, 2024.

Van Cleave, Ryan G. *Travis Kelce: Superstar Tight End.* Capstone Press, 2025.

ONLINE RESOURCES

Visit **www.apexeditions.com** to find links and resources related to this title.

ABOUT THE AUTHOR

Derek Moon is an author and avid Stratego player who lives in Watertown, Massachusetts, with his wife and daughter.

INDEX

ANSWER KEY:
1. Answers will vary; 2. Answers will vary; 3. C; 4. A; 5. B; 6. A